A Little Light from the Stars

A Little Light From The Stars

Revised Edition

A Collection of Stories, Poetry and Essays

Warren Sunkar

Copyright © 2017 Warren Sunkar

The moral right of the author has been asserted.

All rights reserved.

No part of this publication may be reproduced, stored in a retrieval system, or transmitted, in any form or by any means, without the prior permission in writing of the publisher, nor be otherwise circulated in any form of binding or cover other than that in which it is published and without a similar condition including this condition being imposed on the subsequent purchaser.

National Library of Australia Cataloguing-in-Publication entry

Creator: Sunkar, Warren, author.

Title: A little light from the stars / Warren Sunkar.

ISBN: 9780995371613 (paperback)

Subjects: Short stories. Poetry. Essays.

Dewey Number: A820.8

Publishing Consultants: Pickawoowoo Publishing Group

(interior & cover layout)

Thank you to Our Divine Mother

With a dedication and regards to Caroline Cory.

Contents

CREATIVE WORKS ... 1

Great Mother of the Stars ... 2

A Gift from the Stars ... 4

Ayahuasca Dreaming ... 8

My Mate Ed ... 18

Facing Beauty ... 21

A Waltz to Remember ... 23

My Love ... 30

Child of Light ... 33

Refugees of Love ... 41

The Lesson of the Trees ... 43

ESOTERIC ARTICLES ... 45

The New is Here ... 46

Fall On Your Feet…Not On Your Head! ... 51

So, You Want To Be Plastic? ... 57

IT'S ALL GOING A BIT GREY!	61
Sucked In!	69
IT'S ALL GOING A BIT GREY – Part 2	69
Jesus 2.0 The Digital Messiah	75
IT'S ALL GOING A BIT GREY – Part 3	75
Pokemon No!	84
IT'S ALL GOING A BIT GREY – Part 4	84
This Time of Change	91
Open The Window of Grace	98
The Changing of Days, The Parting of Ways	103

CREATIVE WORKS

Great Mother of the Stars

Upon the turning of the great shift of ages,
The darkness writhes, roars, spits and rages.
Humanity trembles in confusion and fear
As we stand upon time's frontier.
Some moments awe inspiring
Other moments terrifying
Our fantastic journey has brought us here.

Oh Great Mother of the stars,
You who have come from afar,
Gently enfolding this world of death
Healing it with your sweet cosmic breath.
In these depths of such travesty
Do you reveal your Divine Majesty.
Universal Queen upon my knees do I pray
As you merge into my being, with your krystalline DNA.
Now a child of Life, Universally reborn
Called to mend the finest of fabric that has been torn.

A Little Light From The Stars

This celestial gown of such radiant beauty.
Guide me to be more gentle,
That I may receive this grace given to me.
The honour of carrying this delicate flame
Divine rose of this heart
How I revere thee!

A Gift from the Stars

On a night of planetary alignment, four of us sat on the balcony of our remote country home.

The starry aurora of the Milky Way glistened spectacularly as we marvelled at the sparkling night sky. Losing ourselves to inward contemplation, we became absorbed into the profound silence pervading the darkness. A zero point of consciousness to which we let go in a deep exhalation. It was here and nowhere, we felt a soft approaching energy that started to enfold and pulsate through us.

For a moment my friend Emerald glanced at me curiously. She then smiled almost expectantly as she shut her eyes to breathe deeply.

From above, in a gentle precipitation of loving energy, a spaceship of indescribable luminous, flashing and pulsing colours descended from the night sky to hover above us.

As we relaxed into the experience, our group consciousness was lifted into a higher frequency and field of soft electrical blue energy. We felt the constraints of our body-bound reality dissolve. Time and space melted into non-existence.

'You are safe…' The words were whispered into our minds.

'You are safe…' Again the words repeated.

Within my deeper being I felt a familiarity with the energies. I could sense true benevolence. A surge of love breathed through the four of us. Our physical eyes closed as we let go to the experience, yet all the while we were keenly aware of each other's presence within a psychic field of resonant unity.

The voice whispered continued assurance. In my mind's eye materialized a celestial being floating before me. A knowing from somewhere deep came to my consciousness; this being was known as Arcturian…

Though the remoteness of this race seemed far removed from earth's reality and experience, through the mind the being and myself began to communicate via an array of words, glyphs and imagery. There was happiness as I was relayed that there had been an important victory in the greater cosmos, yet I also sensed a little sadness in that it might mean some trouble for Earth. Through the exchange I could feel my friends around me in various communions and healing, their hearts pulsating in love for the beneficial energies they were receiving.

Then another surge of love frequency pulsed through my being as I was lifted from my body to their space ship.

The exchanges and downloads became quicker as I was lifted in vibration, feeling plasmic energy wash through me. There was no fear through the entire process – if anything a deep sense of expectation, even longing…

I was aware my friends were still below going through a beautiful process as I raptured into bliss, unable to be related to the conscious mind. Messages were now rapidly encoding my being. What I knew was happening was a healing and reconnection with the thread of universal DNA.

In a sweet void of timelessness, awash in a frequency of bliss I stayed raptured. There is only a blurred remembrance of this experience yet I was deeply and inherently coherent throughout this beautiful process of inwardly familiar cosmic re-orientation. Though time was not experienced in a mundane sense, in earth relativity, it went for hours.

Drifting downwards as lightly as a feather, I was gently reinstated back into time and space. The delicate resurgence of my awareness that I was back in my body had me slowly opening my eyes to see my friends smiling up at the stars with grateful tears in their eyes. Their consciousness had also landed back into their bodies.

My friend Billie looked at me smiling; her heart seemed aglow and pulsing.

The celestial presence began to softly withdraw as the spaceship above us began pulsating. It was about to depart. As we watched, the sky opened above us as we momentarily glimpsed through a wormhole into which the ship was leaving. Beyond this window, there was lightning and flashes of plasmic energy that ominously crackled and rumbled as we glimpsed a tremendous cosmic battle being furiously fought in other dimensions. With a flash the ship left and the vortex dissipated.

Silence fell upon us and we hesitantly looked at each other, in awe and briefly stunned at what we had just seen. It had been a powerful and breathtaking vision.

We then felt a brief return of soft luminescence within our hearts and slowly a deep sense of wellbeing came over us. We laughed and smiled to each other.

We continued for a time staring out into the vastness of the night sky.

Thank you, we whispered to the cosmos, in deep gratitude for the gifts we had received from the stars.

Ayahuasca Dreaming

It was just after sunset and we sat upon the floor.

As I poured the brown liquid I briefly pondered the unexpected synchronicities that had brought us together for such an event. A tingling sensation went through my body and I was aware that the plant was speaking to me. I smiled, we had heard the stories of others and now it was time for an experience of our own.

It was said that the Teacher Plant had a consciousness that would communicate with those who received it with an open mind and heart.

In an unspoken trust we shared a couple of bowls of the brew between us not knowing what to expect and the four of us drank down the bitter potion with distaste.

As the bowls were drained, we lay upon our backs surrendering to a metaphysical journey into the unknown…

Staring at the ceiling, slow, conscious minutes ticked by…

Nestling into the thin mattress underneath me, my sense of self began to gently dissipate into a soft ethereal glow that gently infused me with splashes of warmth that washed through my body.

Rising, dissolving, expanding into greater freedom, my diminishing consciousness of time slowly began dissolving in vapours of love as my awareness of five-sense reality began melting like butter upon a stovetop.

Relaxing, we lightened to become unexpectedly aware of a spritely spirit of earth. Feminine and playful, she darted and hovered between us in a loving and flirtatious dance. Playing with us in a sensual and unabashed manner she caressed all those who were in the room. Diving through the air, she washed herself through me, kissing me on my lips as I laughed in delighted surprise.

I could feel her healing ethereal touches all over my body as her voice whispered beautiful imagery into my mind as my body shivered in blissful response.

I laughed out aloud as she poked my stomach in a soft jest to let me know she could condense and materialise.

As she played, two other kinds of earthen spirits were unveiled and lovingly nestled into my side. I lay on my back stroking them gently as they nuzzled me in a sweet affection.

As I lay there, I could hear and feel my friends around me. Each one was sharing such an experience as the spritely earth spirit swam around the room blessing each of them with her delicious aura that bathed those she touched in kisses of bliss as she whispered visions and voices of love and affirmation.

Shutting my eyes, resting deeper into the experience, the veil of the unseen dissolved before me. We could understand that the Ayahausca plant was a living key and energetic link to that which was the spirit of the earth.

Suddenly, I could feel the ethers above us deeply stir as a dimensional portal opened.

A quickening pulse took me from within and I felt the presence of the Great Guardian.

I looked up as this ultra-terrestrial of light opened the gateway above me to touch my aura with its rainbow of colours and energies.

Unlocking within a deep remembrance, I felt a strong kinship and affiliation with this great multi-dimensional intelligence and I gasped in splendour as this benevolent insectoid drew back the dimensional veils between us and the vibrations of light quickened through the room to engulf us all.

Shutting my eyes, I was raised into an exploding fractal vision of shimmering colours and cascading rivers of pulsing living energies. Waves of ecstasy washed through my body as I launched into the pool of lights around me.

A chameleon of changing vibrations, I shifted gently yet swiftly through the thin veils of dimension. Twirling and spinning in a dance of joy with the ease and grace enlivened from a remembrance, experienced beyond the confines of body consciousness.

Suddenly, I found myself standing in a jungle clearing.

Bright psychic light shimmered all around as exotic birds and insects in symphony adorned the spectacular vision of the world I stood within.

Before me stood four shamans. They were ancient ones, powerful and impressive as they bowed solemnly. Awe inspiring in their headdress of colourful plumage, I bowed in the presence of these teachers. Then in silence we sat in a circle and communed with closed eyes.

I began to fall backwards and upwards into the vast expanse of space as images flashed rapidly through my mind's eye in a collage of information.

I received a forgotten history of secret and dark things. All hidden today behind a movie version of reality, within which we are manipulated and maintained by the nefarious keepers of our world. I cried out in horror as alien beings looked upon humanity with cold, predatory eyes.

A profound sadness took my heart as before me opened a storyboard of tragedy. Holding me in an embrace of love, the Teacher Plant guided me to a deeper understanding of the mostly unseen happenings here upon this Earth.

Humanity's sad history entwined with these greys.

These lost and foreign beings had altered the human race by genetically tampering, implanting and controlling them. Humanity has been not unlike lab rats to these foreign beings and I reeled before the sickening vision of what has happened in humanity's past and what goes on still today from the shadows.

The visions and teachings came with an increasing rapidity which downloaded through my awareness as the Teacher Plant communicated, helping me to understand and remember. I opened further into the experience, trusting the guidance to see the truth of the planetary situation.

The anguish of humanity took my heart as I was expanded to see how humanity was being kept from its true potential. How we are all being manipulated into a vibratory prison with most of the populace unknowing of their fate.

Upon this Earth, all are subject to occult enslavement and are energetically paralysed by those beings that exist outside the now extremely limited bandwidth of humanity's vibratory perception.

I shuddered as I saw within the dark subterranean levels of the planet reptilians hissing from the shadows.

Falling backwards I became aware once again of the presence of my friends.

The greater light pervading the room and us all from within, dissolved any sense of separation as we had all melded as one in psychic unity.

We were as open books to one another and nothing was kept hidden as we accessed each other's thought streams and life waves. Hidden secrets, joys, and fears were shared between us as visual transmissions as the night went on slipping in and out of a timeless blur.

As each of our lives unravelled before one another, they were played out almost cinematically. It enabled us to observe each other's burdens, weaknesses and lives without judgement or condemnation as we all saw from the greater perspective.

We rejoiced in the experience for there were only smiles in such a union as the Teacher Plant guided us all through the moment with a loving embrace.

I became aware of my partner lying upon a couch behind me, beginning to stir, as the Teacher Plant revealed to her that which she found difficult to accept.

Following her energy stream, I opened to her, sharing a vision of great tribulations coming to the planet. She witnessed humanity losing itself to madness and savagery, opening itself to planetary destruction.

She was openly weeping and shaking her head at such a possibility. I was inwardly motioned to go to her. I knelt next to the couch and gently put my arms around her as she burrowed into my chest. Holding her, comforting her, I ran my hands through her hair as she curled foetally, tears running down her cheeks.

As I shut my eyes again a pre-earth remembrance awoke from within both of us.

As stars we flew through space beyond the heavy and suffocating clouds and confines of Earth's density, playing as children of Love. We saw our life threads circling and entwining in a dance of joy and innocence as we felt our connection run much deeper than the short relationship that we share in our earthly personalities.

Then we saw others of our greater family, stars of light, responding to the cry of Gaia and her humanity as we answered in a wave of Love to descend and penetrate into the darkened sphere of Earth, to seed this planet for its birth into its cosmic initiation.

The night sped on as we all throbbed in ecstasy, plunged into a vortex of imagery and unutterable revelation, unfiltered by the limitations of mind.

Each message personal yet shared, each of us taking that which was meant for them. The playful spirit darting and dancing between us all, giving healings and comfort as each of us gasped or laughed at the revelations and messages given them.

Then softly, in an inner dawning of soul stirring and arousing, not unlike a soft crescendo of a playing violin, a haunting song arose within the inner silence and its deep sadness began to take my heart as everything faded into darkness.

Majestic Gaia, like a whale of the ocean depths, was singing her lament through deep space. I was flooded with the deepest of sorrow as her call brought tears streaming down my cheeks. A deep longing rose to my lips as I moaned out aloud in deepest soul pain. Humanity had forgotten their great Mother and she was calling out in her great pain and distress.

As I looked out over Earth in cosmic vision from space,

I knew we were failing her. Great helplessness and shame stirred from within as the acceptance of being part of the collective that was killing her washed through me.

Overwhelmed, I cried and sang back to her through the vast expanse of space.

I was sobbing.

I looked back upon a wayward humanity, out of cosmic rhythm, crippled and poisoned. I cried out to them through space but they were so immersed in themselves that they could not hear.

Humanity, if you would only open and see, you would recoil in horror and shame at the madness you have unleashed. Your loving Mother is in such pain, open your hearts to her for she is part of you and you of her. You have forgotten her sacrifice and how she has laboured for you.

She calls for her children's love and understanding.

As I was launched again through space, a portal opened and in a surge of light and colour I was transported in a neon blur as the great cosmic womb opened before me.

Unable to resist, I merged inside.

Wave upon wave of delightful, mystical energy rippled sensually through me.

I was a solar seed to fertilise and dissolve in liquid ecstasy as my whole body throbbed in deep rhythmical orgasm.

Energy pulsed through me as a cascading shower

that launched through the fountainhead of my crown in unspeakable climax, sparking within and all around me a beautiful fusion in a glorious explosion of light; a conception had taken place.

Crowned in mystical euphoria, a bright rainbow of light shone through me as the Guardian further opened my awareness.

With spurts of energy that flooded through me I was encoded with symbols of living energy like a sun shower of rain.

A living language of glyphs and geometrical shapes awakening aspects of my being to things unknowable to the lower mind.

Slowly, the pulsing began to softly ease as my aura convulsed in joy and fulfilment.

I then began to feel the energy gently leave.

The Guardian and its children slowly withdrew through their dimensional vortex and the consciousness of the Teacher Plant slowly faded from my mind's eye as the realisation of time slowly began to once again infiltrate our awareness.

Our awareness of space grew as we slowly adjusted and settled back to earthly consciousness.

Laying there, glowing, I had cuddled deep into my blanket letting go with a deep, peaceful sigh. Turning around to see smiles beaming from my friends who all just laughed aloud at the experience.

That morning, we all walked outside renewed in life

as the dawning light in a halo of soft pastels christened the horizon before us. The birds in beautiful symphony made music that delighted and raised our hearts as we all greeted the coming day.

Our heightened awareness of the life glowing through us had given us a deeper communion with our Great Mother. Our vibration had been raised as such that I beheld a resonance with Gaia unknown in this short sojourn upon this earth, now understanding her great potential.

With a heartfelt release I thanked the Teacher Plant as I whispered to the horizon.

And I thought…

Humanity, if you would only open your little minds and hearts to embrace your own as children of Life, you would understand. You could enjoy as do birds in their morning celebration, bathing in the light of the spiritual sun.

My Mate Ed

I was sitting on the veranda of my quiet country home, musing with a pen and notepad, watching the kangaroos grazing in the field. Their young ones skipping in delight as the soft light of the sun warmed the Earth. It was a beautiful morning.

Hearing someone walking through the bush, I turned to see my friend Ed approaching the house. In his hands he carried a big blue pumpkin.

'I thought you might like this,' he said with a big smile.

Stepping up onto the veranda, he passed it to me with his earth stained hands. Ed would spend hours in his garden, planting, sowing, watering and reaping. He loved it.

I accepted his beautiful gift, placing it on the table beside me. His eyes glittered all the more knowing his gift was truly appreciated here. He sat down on the chair next to me as we rolled some tobacco, savouring the lovely sun.

'I'll drop some more vegies in this week,' he said in his unique Australian manner.

'The garden has produced so much this season I don't know what to do with it all.'

As we silently smoked, looking out into the paddocks, I pondered on the strangeness of urban living. People walking around in crowded supermarkets, pushing around their shopping trolleys. Packeted food stuffs, genetically modified ingredients, dead fruit and vegetables. A wayward vision of reality that had become so normal to today's Western mindset. Everyone on so many levels had become poisoned with so called 'modern life'.

In my musing I looked over at Ed's pumpkin that seemed to radiate with life and the very love he had nurtured into growing it.

Reading my mind, he spoke.

'You see that,' Ed said pointing to the pumpkin, 'that is real work.' His eyes shone with the intelligence and mischievous undertone of a wood sprite. He chuckled and I smiled, knowing he was also making a soft jest at me and my writing.

We then both seemed to go into a silent contemplation of people living in great cities. The fast pace lifestyles, the pressures and dramas… Those accustomed to a more quiet and natural life could see the vain self-importance of modern urban living, the madness and futility of it all!

I paused in my thought to glance at him. Unable to comprehend the strange and obscure ways of city life,

I questioned out aloud, 'what are they all doing, I don't understand it'?

'You know,' he said with a sincere shrug, 'I don't think they bloody know what they're doing either.'

For a few moments we kept silently pondering. Then we burst out laughing.

He is a funny guy, my mate Ed. The morning flowered into a beautiful country day.

Facing Beauty

I sit facing beauty.
She dances for me in grace and sings to me
with such gentleness that she sings in silence.

She wears a dress of suffering but reveals her
radiance as I glimpse flashes of her nakedness.

In her eyes are the suns and in her smile the
promise of Love eternal, all which she hides
under a veil of death.

But I have unmasked her.
I met her with an open heart and she does
not shy from my stare, for my eyes seek not
to covet something of her.

In such freedom she is a vision of purity that
throws bashfulness to the wind.

Warren Sunkar

In her innocence she reveals all to me
And with her openness I am closed to all else.
And with our separateness, forever we are wed.
In my longing I am fulfilled.

Dance for me forever my maiden.

A Waltz to Remember

On a night of a full moon, gentle spirits were beckoning me to a familiar rock on a small hill that sat overlooking lush fields of a nearby valley. It was upon this rock that I often found solace to sit and contemplate.

As I walked up the hill, the night sky glittered brilliantly.

The moon's silvery white light lit up a path before me, bathing the trees around me in its soft luminescence. The night was still and mystical.

Reaching the top of the hill, I noticed the glow of a small fire on the rock and a shadowed figure sitting silently, staring out into the night sky.

I approached quietly to see an elderly woman wrapped in a light shawl. Her black hair was streaked with silver that seemed to reflect the very starlight sparkling above us. I did not know her ethnicity but glancing at her, it seemed she might have come from any one of the tribes of Earth. There in the moonlight I silently mused, because it felt she might just be all of them.

Her deep black eyes looked out into space. She was unmoved by my approach.

I invited myself to sit next to her so that I could share the glorious view of the star filled firmament.

'Dear old mother,' I said, 'what brings you here this night?'

She turned and looked deep into my eyes. There was an unfathomable depth in her stare. Though she wore the body of an elderly woman, I was in the aura of a powerful spirit.

I stared back at her wonderingly.

I was trying to feel out who or what she was when a voice whispered on the breeze…the Great Grandmother.

A long moment passed. Her presence felt as ancient as the moon.

'I'm not that old,' she said eventually. I knew she was reading my mind. She smiled playfully, and then gave me a flirtatious wink!

I smiled back bashfully. Her deep eyes sparkled as spiritedly as a young child's yet her poise commanded respect as her strong presence overshadowed her aged appearance.

I wondered what was to become of this strange auspicious night. Why had I been led here?

'My dear boy, my sweet child, take my hand,' she said in answer to my thought.

She opened her weathered hand, which I softly took in mine.

There on the hilltop we both shut our eyes.

I was released into a vision of dreaming.

I watched the skies turn quickly, rotating from night to day. I observed the Earth's seasons change in a visual collage of timelessness. I saw continents shift, forests grow and seas change in a flowing graphic of beauty that was played in my mind's eye.

I felt light and buoyant. The vision kept going as I watched in awe.

I saw the journey of humanity throughout the ages. Witnessing the rise and fall of great civilisations and strange things to behold. I observed alien realities manipulating the human race and realised that humanity's long history was far different from what anyone of this modern age could perceive.

The Grandmother Spirit had been there through it all.

As I contemplated what I had just seen, the vision shifted.

I became a little girl walking through a field of flowers remembering the ethereal innocence of a young child as I ran, danced and played.

Upon a storyboard of a feminine life playing out before me, I quickly shifted in years. I became a young teenager staring out under the stars, yearning for love. I felt a young girl's beautiful dreams and high aspirations.

The vision kept going…

I was a young woman finding her first lover…then felt the tears of first heartbreak, the confusion and pain.

I felt courage return and a new love come. I watched the struggles and dramas of an earthly life. Experiencing the birth of my first child, watching my children grow with love and seeing them leave with heartache. I witnessed my life change and my husband grow old in an incessant visual stream of joy and sadness, heartbreak and hope. I felt the cruel touch of time, the ageing of my body.

The tone of the vision shifted again. It became faster…

I felt the loss of loved ones, loneliness and despair. I saw young men recklessly run off to war…images of horror, violence and brutality. I felt the worry of mothers for their children, the yearning of wives hoping for their partners to return; the Earth being destroyed. The madness of the modern world swept around me in a vortex of painful imagery of hopelessness and anguish. It kept going; the vision had become almost frantic.

I reeled and let go of the Great Grandmother's hand to stop the vision.

I felt Grandmother's pain, there was a tear rolling down her cheek.

'I have known many ages…and none has been so strange as this one,' she said."

With a look I questioned her.

I felt the shame.

She looked into my eyes and read my heart. Her face softened and she said in gentle recognition, 'I see you and I are not so different'.

She was gazing into my being, tracing the lines of incarnations and cosmic pre-earth journeys.

I knew what she meant.

The rise and fall of the great civilisations of Earth are nothing but faint ripples upon the ocean of life. The lifetimes of men are but a bauble in space, and all will vanish into nothing but distant memories in the shadows of time.

And what would become of this wayward world?

The glories of so-called modern man are but dust. The vain and the powerful are destined to become but forgotten ghosts. This world civilisation is a towering monument of its disgrace, and here at its end nothing of this age would be left standing. Thus already inscribed upon the ethers was the sad epitaph of this Yuga.

And those of the deep silence had waited patiently throughout it all, watching and calling to humanity to understand and change its ways.

I smiled with a sad knowing and we held each other's gaze in the quietness.

There I pondered for many moments at the strange and wonderful events of this enchanting night.

The breeze had stilled and it was then a thought came to my mind. I rose to my feet.

Inspired, I held out my hand, bowing in a time forgotten chivalry.

Now it was she who stared at me questioningly and wonderingly. I smiled.

Curious, she stood up, taking my hand.

As I brought her to my chest I shared a dreaming of joy, hope and nobility. She looked down at herself, she had become young again. Looking into her eyes I shared a vision of a man looking into the eyes of his first love and together we embraced as we swayed gently together under the stars. We dreamed the healing of the Earth and a new humanity born into an age of wonder, and there we danced through the ages…

After a long and beautiful interlude we gently let go and released.

'Thank you sweet child,' she whispered affectionately.

She leant forward and softly kissed my forehead then turned back to stare out over the moonlit valley.

She smiled as she spoke. 'Now comes the Great Shift of seasons, the one I have waited for all my long years.' There was a sense of expectation and joy in her voice.

We shared the silence staring out to the stars. As the night wore on, sleep began to come over me and my eyes grew heavy. The last vision I had of the Grandmother Spirit was her glowing in silver white and then everything faded into darkness.

I awoke as the first rays of the dawning sun broke through the skies. The fire had become whispers of smoke and she had gone.

Standing up to look over the beautiful sunlit valley, I felt strong and rejuvenated.

A whisper entered my mind and I heard her voice

– 'Grandma has given you a bath!'

I knew I had received a beautiful healing.

I giggled to myself…at such a strange and beautiful night.

It was one I would never forget…

Months later, I was walking through a busy urban street in a major city. Unnoticed by the people rushing about, was an old woman struggling with some shopping bags, trying to navigate the great current of city madness that was all around her. She had tripped up and no one seemed to care.

I walked up to her and offered my hand. She looked up and behind her eyes I saw a familiar glitter.

'My sweet child,' the old lady said and gave me a playful wink.

I helped her to her feet and took her bags.

Together we walked through the urban indifference, smiling.

My Love

Drink, my love
Let your soul have its fill
For the world is a desert and you
Have lost your way.

Rest, my love
You are safe within my arms
Your eyes tell me of your weariness
And I know you are tired of walking in circles.

Cry, my love
Let me weep with you
Let me lighten the burden of your heaviness
For your tears and my tears bleed from one heart.

Pray, my love
I will kneel beside you
Together we will ask the heavens to lessen
the sting of the whipping winds

A Little Light From The Stars

And to send loving rain to cool the scorching
sands that blister your feet.

Strength, my love
Be not thwarted by the fire of the sun,
It tempers the soul
And there are still many more dunes to cross.

Faith, my love
It will lighten your footsteps in the sinking sand
And pick you up when you stumble,
For it is best not to fall in exhaustion when
hungry vultures circle.

Courage, my love
Is to follow the heart and take up your calling
Let it take you beyond this merciless place,
Paradise is waiting.

Do not give up, my love
Here we are but footsteps in shifting sands
For this life is not unlike a dream
And awake you will when you realise
That now is the beginning and end of
Every journey.

Warren Sunkar

        And your purpose?
        It is Love, my love
And when you come home from your long parting
    You will never be separate again.

Child of Light

(A dream of clearing ancestral lines)
Once in the dark forest of my dreams I followed the shade of my father.

In a clouded world of mist and shadows, we journeyed through the gnarled and twisted trees, walking on the path of our ancestors, called Tradition.

We made our way with stealth and hunted with cunning. Felling many a bird from branch and sky, we left a trail of blood and scattered feathers behind us.

As we hunted, I savoured the rare words of praise my father embellished me with as each of my arrows found its mark and I could feel his look of pride upon me with each dull thud of draining life fallen upon the earth; but I could not raise my eyes to meet his stare for, in truth, I hated hunting.

Further he would beckon me into the heavy mists and shadows; foolishly I followed. I dare not question him or his intentions lest his eyes of pride look upon me no longer and he abandon me in this accursed wood. The thought of that frightened me; for often, to myself, I wondered if he knew where we were going at all for as I looked down to my feet to question the path that we were walking, I became fearful and confused because there didn't seem to be one.

Then, after what seemed an eternity of mindless wandering, I could go no further and I stopped. Exhausted, I massaged my aching legs and began to contemplate the senselessness of my actions. Paying no attention to the fearful calls of my father who was yelling at me about the dangers of staying still, I broke down in tears at the pointlessness of it all.

Then, sung out of the darkness, carried upon the dank heavy airs that swirled about us sounded a low and sorrowful moaning. Frozen in my fear, I listened attentively as does a terrified rabbit that listens for the sound of a nearby fox, absolutely still and with a pounding heart. The dreadful cries grew deeper, seeming to reverberate from the very depths of my dark little world- sung with such anguish and hopelessness like a mournful spectre who waits for the light of heavenly acceptance that doesn't come.

Retaining but only a few drops of my evaporated courage, I silently crept through the dense undergrowth towards such misery's source.

From behind a bush I inhaled deeply as I drew back its branches…

Piercing through the dark clouds of my inner world, the forgotten sun shone a ray of Love to illuminate a small forest clearing. In the centre of the clearing kneeled a lone, sadly man. He was a monk. His robes were but rags, they were tattered and torn. His face sullen, his features partially hidden behind a long and thick matted beard on which hung a fine webbing of thin icicles spun by the spinnerets of the ice spider, Frost. His hair, knotted and wild, was tossed back as his tear-filled eyes beseeched the skies for forgiveness. Within his cupped and blood-washed hands he held the crumpled form of a dead white dove which he raised in offering to the heavens.

Held fast, I stared at the scene before me in confusion and fear raced down my spine like the cold hand of a ghost passing through me as I realised the dead dove he held within his hands was one of the birds that I had felled.

His cry came to a sudden stop and my heart skipped a beat for I knew he had sensed our presence. Turning around, he stared directly into my eyes with a gaze so powerful I felt as if the hand of God was around me, able to crush my bones to powder if he so willed it. Rising to his feet, he walked to the edge of the light with the dead, limp dove loosely held within his fingers.

Hypnotised, I was fixed as stone and time was suspended. Then, from the shadows, my father stepped out to protect me, his hunting bow ready and aimed. Breaking the gaze that held me fast, I exhaled sharply for I had forgotten to breathe.

'Step into the light child,' spoke the monk. His tone

soft, his voice was like a gentle song whispered from many different directions and was in great contrast to his deep, powerful eyes that felt like they had stripped me to my essence. Undisturbed by the shade's threatening presence, he ignored my father and kept his eyes stayed on me.

"Step into the light child." He spoke again.

The spirits of uncertainty had stolen my will. Mesmerised, I knew not what to say or do. Sensing my hesitation, his face grew softer and his tone outreaching as he gestured out into the shadows: 'Step into the light child for there are worse things than I out there.'

'What do you want?' I managed to stammer, my voice scared and deflated.

'Fear me not.' His voice was soothing and calm. 'I have come for you.'

Confused, I timidly asked, 'why are you here?'

Keeping me stilled within his gaze he spoke 'For I have wandered through this wood of human misconception for thousands of years, finding the lost and healing the broken-hearted. For thousands of years I have nurtured life within these realms only to have you take it away. This woeful era of senselessness is at its end and now humanity will learn responsibility for itself. It is time to reveal to you a new path; it is time that the children of Earth walk the true way; it is time to lay down your bow and hunt no longer.

He continued: 'I am here because tradition has

become but a path of ignorance and your way has lost its meaning. I am here because in your dreams you are crying for truth. The complacency of aimlessness you have indulged in has become restrictive torture. I am here to tell you to release your grip upon your suffering for it is by your own hand that you strangle yourself. Step into the light child for out there in the shadows there is only slavery. Out there in the darkness of egoism all is illusion.

Struggling with his words I flared up with frustration. 'You would have me lay down my bow and leave me helpless in this savage wood? I say it is you who has lost your way,' I spat back. His words had burned me.

A gentle smile warmed his face. 'Aye, I would have you lay down your bow but you will not be helpless. Verily, I will help make you a giant if you but embrace the truth of who you are. Only in gentleness and compassion can humanity grow, and a giant you will become when you realise that the greatest powers lie latent in the depths of humility.

'For in vulnerability you will find the greatest strength.

And understand you will that the finest armour is openness and only in obedience will you find true freedom.'

'You speak to me in riddles,' I shot back, confused.

'Nay, it is your life that has fallen into riddle,' he replied. 'I offer its solution. Here in the ray of heavenly Love, the shades of perception disappear within the light of Truth. Here all darkness is vanquished.'

Silenced, I tried to absorb all that he was saying.

His face dropped in sadness as his eyes swelled with tears. Holding the dead bird forward, cupped in his bloodied hands, he softly spoke: 'She is of you, yet you know it not.'

Confused, I stammered, 'she is just a bird.'

And he answered sadly: 'Child of Earth, would you stay blind? If this is just a bird, then this is but a dream and I will bid you farewell for it is your choice to remain in the darkness.'

Despair welled within me and panicked, I pleaded: 'Please don't leave me.'

Gesturing the bird towards me he whispered: 'She is of you child and she is more than just a bird, understand that; she is the delicate flame of inspiration blown out by the breath of ignorance; she is love pierced by a dart of thoughtlessness; she is an unanswered prayer, fallen back into the void.'

Tears streamed down his face as he explained softly: 'With each life that you claim, you kill part of yourself. With each step further into darkness you take, the colder you become.' Pleading, he reached out his hand and asked: 'Lay down your bow child, take my hand; it is time to end this foolishness.'

I went to walk to him but my father hissed, his bow raised in protection, keeping me behind him.

The monk turned toward the shade and with authority spoke: 'Be gone illusion of yesterday, you will lead no more. Be gone minion of fear, you are but a shadow of what is because your way is lost in what has been. The children of Earth will be deluded no longer.'

As the monk continued, the shade began to tremble. 'Let you not make your child stand behind you, but you behind your child for it is through children that life expresses itself. Life is eternal progression and renewal, it cannot be stayed. So I say unto you, that he who tries to stay life with the hand of ignorance will be thwarted by himself, for he acts contrary to his own true nature; and he who holds back the children of Life is fear of Life itself. Be gone!'

Then, with a firm gaze and gesture he dismissed my father. Powerless, the shade lowered his bow and resigned subserviently, stepping back into the shadows behind me.

Turning back to face me, the monk's eyes looked at me deeply. 'In truth, all fathers are but children following in the footsteps of their own. Had you true sight you would have seen your father as a child, being beckoned onwards by his own fear and then realised the disastrous plight of humanity, that it is lost and walking in circles. Such is the foolishness of man. I have seen sons bury their fathers to be buried by their sons in a grim procession of eternal death. It is to be no longer, the cycle of ignorance ends with you.

'Step into the light child, it is Love. Lay down your bow and embrace me for I am eternal Life.'

Drawing upon my courage, I laid down my bow and, taking a step forward, I accepted his hand. Leaving the darkness of my lower nature, I stepped into the light. Behind me I could hear the shade crying out in desperation and fear – it was repentant and frightened but I did not look back. I was beyond its grasp and I knew all was to be forgiven.

Absorbed into the light I was met in Love as I embraced my divine self and, in a flash of union, we became One. There in the light of Truth, all darkness was vanquished and the flame of ecstasy raced through me as tears of joy streamed down my face. Raising the dead white dove I held within my fingers, I brought it to my lips. There in the light of understanding, I gently kissed it with the breath of Life and released it into the air…

That day, in the forest of my dreams, a lone white dove spiralled into the sky higher than any arrow could reach her. Her cries of freedom and love echoed throughout my world, causing all the trees to yield up their birds into the sky. Leading them up into the heavens, she pierced through the dark clouds of obscurity that had always been there and the divine sun broke through in brilliant colour and unutterable revelation. I fell to my knees in tearful bliss; never would I be lost again.

I had found Love divine.

Then I woke up…

(Written at age twenty-two)

Refugees of Love

We sat silently around a campfire. My friend Jahve gently strummed his guitar in a sweet melody that seemed to evoke Life and dance in our hearts.

The spirit of the small mountains where we were staying was kind and feminine. She visited us with a whisper in our minds, pleased to know we could receive her and that we respected the sacred area. It was beautiful to feel welcome as we sat around the fire in a meditation with her.

My friend Emerald gently swayed to the soft music. Her deep eyes glinting, reflecting the light of the stars.

'The *new* is singing to us,' she said as her beautiful smile shone with the radiance of the warm fire before us.

I looked into the night sky. I knew what she meant. The times were changing rapidly.

Those of us awakening to the new reality were contemplating the greater cosmic drama that was unfolding before us. Lives had been changed forever…

The fire crackled. The scent of the trees and flowers permeated the surrounds with a unique Australian aroma.

Pondering the events of the past months, she spoke. 'If I would speak of what has transpired over these last months, I don't think anyone I know would believe me.'

Our friend Billie laughed softly. 'I don't think anyone could understand you,' she said 'The timelines are cleaving and the old world is failing. Those who cannot hear…it's best to leave them be.'

I smiled, knowing the thoughts of my friends, their realisation of greater Life and their remembrance of their place amongst the stars. The *new reality* was already present. Here was the new seed of Earth and before my eyes it was already flowering.

Emerald continued: 'The life that I once lived has become a fading dream. Its sickness apparent. The mindlessness of a civilisation so wrapped up in itself. It was never meant to be…'

We all contemplated the fading dream of the dystopic reality we were leaving. The spirit of new life was pervading our hearts; we were upon the shore of the New World.

'I don't think I could ever go back,' Emerald mused.

We all pondered what she said silently for a while.

After a deep pause Billie asked, 'would you really want to?'

'Naaaaah…' Emerald exclaimed loudly, as we all started laughing.

A shooting star lit up the night sky above us.

We just smiled at each other as the heat of the fire radiated upon our bodies within our warm circle of love.

The Lesson of the Trees

Children of Adam, you too grow with light,
the light of Love.

How you struggle amongst the weeds
thinking they are your brothers when they
are your death.

Do not be afraid to stand on your own for
blessed is the tree that stands tall within an
empty field.

And blessed is the tree that bathes in the light
of the loving sun for it has found Truth and
does not wither before it.

Go children of Adam with this lesson of the trees.
Let it be your seed and grow tall in God.

ESOTERIC ARTICLES

The New is Here

Today, new Life energies are entering our planetary system and our awakening population truly needs to review its current mindset as to how it has defined its existing 'reality'. These cosmic rays of healing and dissolution are forcing a shift in current belief structures that have dominated the human collective for millennia.

Light is being shed in all places and people are called to retrace and re-interpret many events, beliefs and assumptions that have inhibited their true spiritual growth and alignment. Understand, the current intervention of these cosmic energies is an opportunity to resolve and heal various schisms and fractures within our personal and collective being.

We are in fact, multidimensional beings that are fast coming into remembrance of our true divine heritage.

While the new energies are an extension of Love and Grace from our Divine Creator, our unprepared population will undergo much unnecessary trauma if it fails to recognise and accommodate this great wave of divine Love which is now growing in intensity. The great change of the age is upon us and many are experiencing its tangible effects.

Here is some sound advice to all those adamantine minded and resolute intellectual pillars of 'modern society', per-haps it is over-time to reverse-engineer your current beliefs and mind constructs. If you are brave enough, you will discover and let go of the tangled mess of contradictions, illusions and buried insecurities you have raised your flag on.

If you trust a little more in Life and you might just find this period one of amazing healing.

Understand that for many, what is perceived as 'reality', is but a set of self-generated agreements and contracts with our multidimensional environment. While we have the potential to awaken and heal each other, certain belief structures can also limit and define what we experience in our given reality. Such is the pathology of our modern technocratic and materialist culture. As we continue to mutually condition each other, most of humanity is today resisting the incoming new life encodings and many are entering an entropic and dystopian state that is leading to a disaster with severe cosmic implications!

With the new energies entering and the subtle planetary grid reforming, the parameters of our earthly experience are being drastically redefined. Today we have the potential and unique opportunity to embrace a more expansive multidimensional reality. New life encodings are being received by those who have been selflessly attentive as 'life as we have known it' now expands into an energetically regenerative and infinitely multiplying experience of unfolding multidimensional consciousness.

How we experience the coming period will be our decision – if we consciously engage or deny these new energies and processes. It could possibly be one of genuine revelation, or the purging of resistant and opposing realities from the planet.

As the planetary healing gets under way the great schisms within our collective and personal paradigms are now being brought to the surface to be resolved.

Perhaps it is pertinent to look at a few basics.

In Western society, most of our current laws, social ethics, workplaces and institutions are nothing but a contrived extension of collective indoctrination that occurred during our schooling years. These schooling systems have neglected our true psychic and spiritual heritage and relay nothing but a programed and fractured version of reality given by certain authorities that have enormously contributed to a great contortion and confusion within our given holistic reality.

If you don't believe this, then simply look at the results.

The amount of waste and poison that humanity produces, our serious neglect in regards to our subtle or spiritual realities and modern society's lack of genuine creativity. This has all resulted in an inability to truly resolve the deep sickness and problems that have taken hold of humanity and the planet.

All of this has only served the misplaced purpose of keeping people separate and chained to a dominating and distorted mindset, which has held most people locked up in an artificial and greatly limited construct of time and space reality. The result has been a lot of wasted time and resources with the creation of many materially bound pseudo-sciences and philosophies.

Not to take away from many sincere and aligned educators out there but one can plainly see that when a civilisation begins to oppose its own biological and spiritual foundations, not only is it fighting a losing battle, it is losing itself to soul death.

The only things such a civilisation can look forward to is growing madness, vampirism and war.

Many surprises are in store and today humanity is awakening to those control mechanisms which have been placed over them for millennia. The incoming energies are revealing a multidimensional and cosmic reality that is now exposing hidden systems of enslavement and manipulation that will reveal the true inherent nature of our current socially dominating transhumanist reality.

Let it be seen that often, we as a society, have been the accomplices in our planetary destruction and takeover through ignorance, selfishness and misplaced intentions.

However, the *new* is arriving and with it comes profound change. The great divine intervention is here to restore our true cosmic planetary alignments, and humanity is today being reawakened to its divine origins.

Our path has always been a living one and we cannot enter new territory dragging our heavy loads from an outdated paradigm and expect to be fine.

These incoming energies will redefine the human race but if we hold on and identify with outdated belief structures they will only pull us into further confusion as the new manifests.

We are being called to let go of our mundane attachments to allow the intelligent new life to redirect us safely from a path that is degenerate and destructive.

If we can embrace the *new* we will find that this time can be one of true ascending realities and ultimately, divine union.

Fall On Your Feet...Not On Your Head!

Our physical material world holds true potential as to our divine soul unfoldment as a species, as well as contortions and distortions as to the nature of our collective journey through these realms and cosmos.

People need to wake up and pay attention for if we as a race seek to inherit our true divine birthright, it is important for people to question the direction in which we seem to be 'travelling'. This includes the possibility of contorted future incarnations as a collective into the 'realities' we are ourselves co-scripting.

Sometimes to see where we are going, one needs to know where they stand.

Ancient allegories, myths and stories have often related to humanity a collective event alluding to a fall of our collective being into realms that we as a race were premature to experience or possibly not even meant for.

Today, many people are realising that somehow and at some point humanity shifted into identification with this physical material reality which is very far removed from the reality of our divine pre-history.

Gnostics have often hinted that what we perceive as the physical universe is in fact a realm in which humanity remains for the most part captive through a state of relativity and misidentification.

Through wrongful identification with our shadow selves (the personality/carnal nature/lower self) and misunderstanding the resonate field we exist within (duality), humanity has been able to deeply complicate its predicament by misuse of its forces and intelligence. Thus has the domination of our lower collective nature continued to involute to an ever deepening distortion of our 'reality'.

What has become known as *The Fall* still continues today!

As we seek to hold onto form life through our attention and identification at the expense of our divine nature, so do we corrupt our true divine potentiality.

The deeper complexities we will not get into in this piece! This is a somewhat simple explanation to a problem with real complexity and is but a loose conceptual framework to cast a little insight and light as to the extension of troubles we find ourselves in within our current collective situation.

However, despite what seems an impossible situation, divine servers have always subscribed that humanity does have a divine pedigree, and through our intrinsic nature we have the possibility to reconnect with our true divine reality and reawaken our divine beingness within this given organic matrix. Then through a transmutational and transfigurative process, we can move essentially to our original and destined vibratory reality.

Unknown to many upon the planet, this process has been happening throughout the ages by certain personages and groups who have embarked upon *The Way* and gone home. The teachings of the Avatars have been proclaimed throughout humanity's collective history and the way lived by those astute enough to heed the inner call of their true divine nature.

Today, should those of humanity heed their divine calling they will find they have their own inner co-ordinates and capability to transcend the current situation with much assistance from divine intermediaries and intelligence! Engaging consciously and actively as participants in the *True* divine plan.

The purpose of this piece is not to inspire theological debate but to open inquiry as to our true nature and the importance of gaining a deeper perspective of where we are, what we are and where we might go – especially if we continue with our collective unconscious momentum and movement towards a transhumanist 'reality' that in truth, most of humanity has no clear inner perspective of.

As we neglect to heed true inner divine knowing and proceed to venerate matter and form we continue to involute and reflect ever distorted realities back upon ourselves. In misusing our creational abilities we have the real potential to take ourselves further into realms far from our true divine reality and into states that are very hard to come back from.

To date, humanity has been aided by Divine Intelligence, enabling humanity to understand its time and space predicament, and through its evolutionary capacities and sympathetic organic matrix enable it to find its way back home to its true divine cosmic origins. Our natural organic reality provides us with the means and opportunity to reawaken our divine potential and go the way home. However, through the domination of the lower mind and the misuse of our creative abilities, we lose our way and we now see a miscreant humanity seeking the total augmentation, control and blatant destruction of its organic reality.

Today's transhumanist 'reality' is but the deeper contortion and inversion of the true divine path and is but a signpost for a very hard and long journey back to our true divine home.

In these lower worlds we are subject to crystallisation, degeneration and 'I' sentiency. The concretion and adaptions of the lower mind lead to fundamental distortions as to our true soul identification and nature. With the loss of our inner knowing we are mostly unable to discern *The Path* and thus are subject to many confusions and distortions.

Today, society is experiencing an incessant push towards a transhumanist reality and new world order by certain individuals, groups and governments. As to the full agenda of these people who are guiding us towards these ends, we are as a race still relatively in the dark. Their tactics of subliminal manipulation, by-passing democratic processes and inhumane enforcement indicate their corruptive intent. The world ego with its 'established authorities' seeks to circumvent our inherent birthright having themselves misplaced their own identification with divine unity and lost themselves to involute pathways.

However today, due to the stimulation of the Earth and humanity by certain cosmic energies, we are gifted with the possibilities of understanding and working with these in-flooding divine intelligences to co-creatively assist humanity with its re-identification to its true divine primordial unity! We have the potential to awaken from our misaligned perspectives into which we have fallen and to assist in the *True* divine corrective process.

Here we need to shift our identification from our own personalised realities to our true soul nature.

Our biology and genetic potentiality flourish under the arriving waves of divine Love, awakening the consciousness of humanity. These new encodings are seeding the receptive, and new life is emerging. This is today being played out through the intensifying dramas of the world ego.

Warren Sunkar

It is time to embrace the change and your true inner potential...

So, You Want To Be Plastic?

Artificial Intelligence is alien and foreign pathology used to augment the primordial essence of the archetypal creative behaviour and alchemical force.
   *(*Sadiki Bakari, *Hip Hop Androids, Artistic Clones And the Portal of Artificial Intelligence)*

We live in a time of accelerated processes due to the great stimulation of new cosmic energies entering our planet. For those who are intuitive and truly receptive, this moment offers a portal of tremendous opportunity in terms of spiritual awareness and growth as cosmic energies and divine intelligences birth humanity into a paradigm of meta-knowledge and multidimensional reality.

However, if these vibratory encodings and living energies are not consciously assimilated by the race, then ultimately a reversal in terms of consciousness and spiritual potentiality takes place. Today, we can clearly observe that most of humanity is plummeting further into involutional consciousness and reality.

Unfortunately, in a time of true spiritual opportunity and crises we are truly witnessing a planned subversion of the human life field into a lower density and psychic distortion. An involution of reality that if embraced cannot be supported or even attended by certain divine intelligences who presently assist humanity for a long time to come.

Have you heard more and more talk lately about the subject of transhumanism?

If you haven't as of yet, you will soon. Because today we see the agenda and its implementation arising before us with breathtaking speed!

It seems that biologist Julian Huxley possibly first coined the term *transhumanism* in the late 1950s, defining it as 'man remaining man, but transcending himself, by realizing new possibilities of and for his human nature'.

Like Hitler and the Nazis, it seems that transhumanism today has become a way to attempt to create so-called superhumans or gods through scientifically enforced programing, genetic manipulation and the augmentation of humanity's organic and spiritual processes and realities!

It seems that certain members of the human race seek to hijack humanity into their theories and relativities of what they deem evolution!

Currently our schools and learning institutions are being subverted to embrace such programing, and increasingly through the media we are now continually being bombarded with subliminal messages and themes that seek to steer the collective's consciousness towards this end. The very use of such subversive tactics upon the collective clearly shows that those who are steering humanity in this direction have an agenda.

The rise and incessant push of GM foods, virtual reality, cybernetics and geo-engineering is today becoming obvious. Undoubtedly, this will come at the expense of our own innate and natural potentialities.

One here is not talking about fearing science, change or 'progress' but simply indicating that humanity as a whole should look much deeper into understanding its innate and spiritual realities before embracing such 'solutions'.

Technocracy is in truth nothing but a pseudo-science and philosophy. It is spawned by the collective's ignorance of its true divine purpose and rejection of its true spiritual identity.

When embraced by humanity, a transhumanist reality is an innate and collective soul death. As humanity falls further from the true world soul to embrace inorganic imitation, it will only open itself further to collective psychosis and possession. This is today being clearly exhibited by those so-called elite who have fallen deeply into involutional practices and theories.

With simple observation one can see that the merging of our spiritual and organic realities with synthetic materials, coarse electromagnetic frequencies and inorganic substances is but an obvious and severe contortion of the human psyche as well as a big step down in vibratory reality.

Our inner spiritual and organic technologies are far more superior in contrast to that which current materialistic science would have us perceive as 'technology'. Our subtly constructed bodies and inherent processes enable us to transcend our current material, third-dimensional experience, giving us the possibility and probability of true spiritual ascension. They are being raped and interfered with.

Your unmolested human genetics and true archetypal blueprint offer the possibility for true divine incarnation. Do you think such synthetic constructs of mind, imprinted emotional responses, virtual realities and cybernetics can efficiently replicate such opportunity and possibility?

Of course not!

This all lies beyond the scope and sight of pseudo-science and the materialist or 'technohead'. They are unable to perceive or fathom the depths of humanity's spiritual realities from which they have far fallen.

While many people may look out into today's rising technocratic 'reality' with wonder and even awe, they are in fact witnessing humanity's true spiritual death!

Such a 'reality' can only seem appealing to an inhumanity!

So, you want to be plastic?

IT'S ALL GOING A BIT GREY!

The vortex of personality capture is not just for counterintelligence, biometrics and spying. It is also for possible mind clones and virtual avatars with or without your permission.
  Sadiki Bakari, *The Magnum Opus*

With the ongoing and multifarious changes precipitated by the influx of new Aquarian energies, the coming period will yield many surprising dramas and events within humanity's personal and collective paradigms.

With new light encodings triggering multidimensional awareness in many, people will not only have to reconsider their own roles in how they interface with Mother Earth but also become aware of other intelligent life in many diverse forms. This includes beings of nefarious intent who have been manipulating reality as we know it from their 'hidden spheres'.

While many beings from many realities, cosmic and terrestrial, are here to assist humanity in its transition, there are also other alien realities here for more sinister purposes. As many awaken from their third-dimensional slumber this is important to address as it might catch some people unawares and definitely should be mentioned in the light of humanity's race towards a technocratic future.

Today, it is no secret that humanity has been manipulated and exploited by certain elite and ruling families for generations. What is being revealed here is how they have been working compliantly and/or subconsciously with beings from an alien origin.

The 'transhumanist agenda' pointed to by many writers and speakers, is well advanced across the globe. A plethora of Hollywood movies and television series over the past couple of decades, such as *Lucy*, *Transcendence*, *The Matrix*, *Ex Machina* and many others – seemingly fantastic to the eyes of those empathically divorced from nature and their soul realities – are in fact embedding into the collective consciousness a potential technocratic prison that has multidimensional ramifications.

One here would point out that it is strange that many people scoff at the mention of divine and subtle realities but are all too willing to accept an alternate digital version of reality, into which they are fast being herded!

As new cosmic energies reveal our multidimensional ancestry and reality, humanity will come into contact with certain entities that have today become known as the 'Greys'. These alien beings work from more subtle dimensions of 'reality' and have a nefarious investment in what is happening to humanity within this moment of collective awakening.

We will not, in this piece, go into their history but attempt to explain how they are very much the manipulative hand behind today's transhumanist encroachment!

Many people have mixed feelings about our progressively rising technocratic society, though it seems for many it has already been sold as the way humanity should go. Hollywood propaganda, government regulation in education, medicine, welfare and other areas as well as one's own addictions to social media and computer gaming, are steadily forcing upon our organic world a designed inorganic circuitry to which we are being attuned. An elaborate digital paradigm that often seems to many a more attractive alternative to the rather sick and mundane world that so many people's lives have become.

It is this 'attunement' principle I would like to highlight in this piece.

We in our cities are being fast surrounded by an electronic digital world.

More spiritually inclined and aware beings are conscious of the subtle bodies they possess. These bodies we construct through our alignments, thoughts and energetic exchanges with various realities. Now, with many people attuning to digital frequencies, I would ask if they can conceive it possible to enter a world entirely fabricated and engineered by a nefarious intelligence simply through this process of collective attuning.

Unfortunately, after certain multidimensional experiences of late, this writer says a definite 'yes'.

In fact this digital world already exists!

In the Disney movie *Tomorrowland* we have a group that has been able to create an alternate digital world. This is how they attempt to 'save humanity' from impending disaster. This world is a projected frequency, which is implied through this film and others of its kind to be projected from the moon, offering a seemingly fantastic reality which seems considerably more marvellous than our seemingly mundane and danger-fraught 3D reality. However, nothing is spoken about the cosmic and spiritual ramifications of this alternate reality and also the possibility that this 'new world' could be controlled by darker alien intelligence!

It *is* possible that a person's consciousness is able to slip into this virtual world or even be harvested after death having attuned themselves to it for most of their lives. Energy follows thought and this is done through constant interplay with artificial intelligence and digital reality. Many people in the cities are disconnected from their organic-spiritual matrix and are unable to understand the implications of this subversion. In fact, most are quite happily *participating in it*!

Already on subtle dimensional planes we are being interfered with by certain subtle tech devices developed by hostile intelligences and implanted with nano-technology unnoticed by those who are unable to awaken to subtle frequencies. However, it seems a correctly focused being can expel such tech from his subtle bodies as they are of a more refined matter but it will now become obvious why we are being 'chem-sprayed', why nanotechnology is appearing in food and why they are pushing the microchip agenda.

Attuning our gross and subtle bodies to certain frequencies as we continually interact with this technocratic world will subvert the collective human life field into an alternate prison reality!

As fantastic and surreal as this sounds this *is* what is taking place on Earth today and they are a lot closer to achieving this goal than what most people think. I have been shown whole populations that have been subverted in this manner by the Greys.

Yet it goes deeper with the understanding that Earth herself has been under attack by such technology through various satellite and space stations as well as the rewiring of her surface through various means and methods. Humanity, by developing smart grids, Wi-Fi technology and even creating certain building monuments, has been complicit in her torture and capture. The people have also become their own keepers and maintainers of their technocratic prison with few wanting to look at alternative viewpoints of the reality we are all experiencing.

Another consideration is that with the awakening and

access to many multidimensional frequencies the Greys have developed their own technologies to interfere with, piggyback on or highjack certain frequencies to suit their own agenda. While attuning to divine or higher frequencies, an awakening being can be confronted by an off-planetary or interplanetary signal or frequency that is not from a divine or higher source and can become confused, or their processes distorted and interrupted. Today this is being experienced by those awakening to their new genetic light encodings and who are accessing extra-planetary information and energies.

The Greys have also created certain technologies to interfere with subconscious and dreaming states to alter people's emotions and experiences, and in this way affect people's moods in daily life or even rewire their subconscious processes.

I would also like to mention that the introduction of virtual reality headsets is a means of total disconnection from our subtle planetary grid. Our biological brain has many subtle connections and receivers to our planetary grid and cosmic intelligence, through which an awakening being experiences many multidimensional layers of reality and communication. Artificial electrical impulses and exposure to virtual reality headsets will in fact damage these subtle receivers and mess with our etheric antennae, possibly doing irreparable damage. It should be acknowledged that in recent years certain government and independent papers have been found and exposed to the public, revealing certain entities in the world who are attempting to manipulate and control the collective human mind through external conditioning programs and technologies.

I have highlighted in previous pieces that cosmic evil needs human hands to implement its agenda to subvert the collective life field of humanity. This is done through programing systems and creating planetary confusion and fear to which so many researchers, such as Sadiki Bakari and David Icke, testify. The agenda is to divert humanity's current planetary awakening and birth at its crucial phase of development!

People should understand that with the current and ongoing planetary awakening and re-connection with the subtle energy grid of the planet to our cosmic divine origins, many of our current technologies will soon become redundant and replaced by suitable, subtle and more cosmically compatible means, in tune with universal harmony.

The new cosmic energies that are being experienced by many will provide new definitions of reality, awakening our dormant biological and spiritual faculties to a heightened and benevolent state of interacting with our environment. Truly, Mother Gaia's treasure chest of love and knowledge has not even been touched by modern humanity as we begin to expand even beyond her borders, interfacing with benign and beautiful cosmic intelligence!

Many people testify that thought creates much of our experiences of reality. If humanity persists in denying the incoming light and information, seeking to live at the expense of higher truths and ignore the obvious corruptions of the world to sell out for personal comfort and selfishness, then certain malevolent beings will provide the means for their choice.

A hyper controlled, self-generated alternate reality that is the ultimate lie!

Many in this world are today experiencing new frequencies of Light and everything is changing fast. This is a call for people to leave the Babylon matrix that threatens to suffocate us all. Those who are awakening are realising that within this phase of the planetary shift we are being assisted by certain divine beings who have today come very close to Earth. We must look within, discern and make the necessary shifts to accommodate the new divine energies that are now entering our planet.

Sucked In!
It's All Going a Bit Grey – Part 2

Many people today still laugh at the very idea of extra-terrestrial intelligence. They laugh even harder at the suggestion of an alien intelligence that is rumoured to control and manipulate the planet. However, for an increasing number of people today, in light of what is being revealed across the planet, this has become a very real possibility.

The global shift in consciousness is under way, and with the flood of new Aquarian energies triggering multidimensional awareness in many, humanity itself will soon come to the collective realisation that we are definitely not alone in the universe.

Even though many writers and speakers have pointed to this possibility, taking much scorn and ridicule from the public, it does not take much research and reasoning to surmise this as a possible reality. Like it or not, the coming period will bring about such a change in consciousness that it will be up to us to assimilate this possibility as we unfold into its probability!

Full disclosure will probably not come from government authorities but from our own collective realisation and remembrance.

My intent is merely to provide a guiding hand as humanity shifts into multidimensionality and takes up its position as an outpost of Light in this universe. With many veils now dissolving, these writings are given to assist an awakening race as we move rapidly towards the greater shift. The coming rending of the veil between dimensions will be swift, and to understand what is unfolding it is best to be as prepared as we can for this impending transition.

I have talked previously that in order to manifest its plans, a certain nefarious alien intelligence needs to embed them within humanity's collective consciousness to bring about their manifestation, and how Hollywood film is often used for this purpose.

In the movie *The Golden Compass* we have an elite group called the Magisterium trying to control the planet by preventing knowledge of humanity's cosmic connections to the greater universe. They invent a technological means by which they separate a being's personality from its soul. Placing a young child in an electric cage and through an undisclosed means of frequency, light and electricity, they literally cut off the child's soul connection. I would like to say that this is an analogy of a collective process which is well under way today.

As was explained in the first part of this piece, humanity continues to enclose itself in an EMF/digital prison. As we ourselves are electromagnetic beings, such distortive and imposed frequencies can alter and disrupt certain inherent cognitive processes, alter our physical chemistry and damage our subtle and biological receptors, creating major impediments not just to our physical health but also to our current collective process.

We are in the advancing stages of cosmic reconnection as the subtle planetary grid is now being re-aligned with our true divine source. This complex energetic matrix is also what transmits certain cosmic and divine energies, intelligence and encodings to our individual and collective being. The implications of an activated worldwide satellite-Wi-Fi network are nothing but a disguised attempt to interfere with these energies and encodings, damaging and entrapping our Earth Mother as well as imprisoning humanity through frequency manipulation. The Greys, in their understanding of how humanity is energetically connected to Earth, seek to further corrupt the reforming planetary grid which has been achieved in the past in their attempts to shut down the human race. The distortive and interfering frequency through satellite-Wi-Fi technology is seeking to corrupt our higher biological mutation into the new light frequency which many of us are now experiencing.

Mother Earth is a living being who is today going through her own catharsis. She is being attacked incessantly by alien intelligence. Those people who have maintained a connection to Earth or who are today attuning to the new planetary configuration can see the severe effects such technology is having on her!

The growing electro-magnetic frequency barrier is not only keeping us from connecting with our greater cosmic intelligence but it is also repelling many benevolent cosmic beings who are here to assist us at this point of our planetary transition.

Through my personal experience, it seems the Greys' direct interface with humanity occurs in the state between the frequency range of waking and asleep. This suggests why technologies such as our televisions and monitors are emitting at certain frequencies and why through technological interfacing they want most of our collective consciousness sustained within this spectrum. This keeps humanity in a semi-hypnotic state, creating energetic bonds and karma within their controlled frequency bandwidth. They are capturing our collective mind and soul, collecting data to create mind files and 'avatars' in an attempt to subvert our consciousness into digitised inorganic bodies. This is how in the past the Brothers of Shadow were able to capture beings through a form of manipulation using certain lucid dreaming techniques.

It is also why human agents controlled by the Greys' are put through MK Ultra techniques, brain fracturing and military training, which are in essence the same thing!

They need to keep us fractured or in a state of semi-slumber so that we become more adept and familiar to living in our misaligned subtle bodies rather than grounded in our true spiritual centre. This is done through the attuning of our subtle bodies to a digital frequency environment. It is all about consciousness transference as witnessed in so many films in Hollywood today. Within this controlled frequency range they have certain subtle technologies that can be used to further infiltrate us. Once digital avatars of people have been created in their generated virtual reality world, which have been aligned and calibrated to the personality (done through created mind files given by the people themselves through various social media), the consciousness can be tricked to transfer into this digitised body.

What one is trying to make people aware of here, is that although the internet has provided an expeditious means of accessing and transferring information so valued by the 'Truther Community', it is the very time spent within the portal of interfacing through artificial intelligence that is the problem. We must understand this energetically – its controlled and manipulated frequency is the energetic wormhole to a virtual reality prison. In a state of constant engagement and attunement, our psyche and subtle bodies are actually being reconfigured and captured within a frequency range which will subvert our consciousness into the digital avatars of ourselves!

Basically, the longer we spend interfacing through AI and the more energy we give to this portal, the more it will consume us regardless of whether one holds the belief they are helping the world or not. We are talking here of a complete subversion of the collective consciousness into a virtual reality world...that already exists!

It is happening very quickly.

Understand that with the new planetary awakening and alignment happening today, many people are experiencing subtle shifts into a true unified awareness and decentralisation of consciousness which enable greater empathic and latent gifts of Spirit to be quickly recollected. In order to engage this process we must let go of artificial means of interacting and interfacing with our living environment. People will experience the awakening of their own dormant spiritual and biological capacities, eliminating the need for such reliance on artificial intelligence.

The choice is yours as to which reality you wish to embrace.

Jesus 2.0 The Digital Messiah
It's all going a bit grey – Part 3

Your imagination is now cyber traveling inside of the synthetic computation of computer programs, computer software and holographic forms of reality. Instead of your imagination and mind being nurtured, it is melodically being hacked and infiltrated.
Sadiki Bakari, *The Magnum Opus*

There is no doubt humanity is at a very vulnerable stage in its collective transitional phase into the Aquarian Age. People are confused and bewildered as the veils lift and we recognise the madness of those authorities that seek to control us.

We as a race are threatened with tearing ourselves apart. Even within the so-called Truther Community, maddening idealisms, confusion and emotive reactions govern the stage. Due to a lack of true knowledge of the human condition, which is even distorted and confused by those more admirable researchers and seekers of truth, we have worked our way into a growing tension and confusion that seems to benefit the very nefarious beings that we are trying to escape from!

In this piece I would like to highlight that one here doesn't put the blame solely on the illuminati, aliens and entities etc. Humanity as a whole has also made some very poor choices in the past century. Many have known for decades that the direction in which we were heading was wrong and many chose to ignore the numerous warnings sounded. In lives of selfishness, we ourselves invoke much of the very darkness that we experience. We are not helpless beings as so many people today suggest…we have a divine heritage and we are children of Love, even if most of us have forgotten this. Some of us have not.

As the intensifying light clarifies the shadows around us and despite what seems a darkened time to many, we are now in a time of our collective divine emergence and I would have humanity not forget this!

However, what is also emerging today is that over past decades while we have fed ourselves on junk television, junk food and selfish distractions, those who have been in places of authority have only been too happy to oblige us. This they have been doing while advancing their own agendas, building an arsenal of technologies in conjunction with certain alien races that will lead to our demise. Today we have been dumbed down and fractured, to be brought to our knees. While intellectuals have argued against many so-called conspiracy theories, time and time again things assumed insane and ludicrous only decades ago have become reality. It seems today such people are becoming a little more hushed as they are now beginning to see the truth of what is unfolding before their very eyes!

Normally my writings are not so personal, however in the light of what is being revealed in these pieces, I thought others could benefit from my personal experience.

Just a month ago (May 2016) I was put through some very hard and disturbing multidimensional attacks which lasted for about 10 days. They came rather unexpectedly, were quite furious and to put it simply, were designed to 'literally take me out'.

However, through this attack I sensed a divine hand keeping me guided through these experiences which had me emerge, relatively safe and sound, although a little sore and shaken. These events were witnessed by several people who can and will corroborate the experience.

The first parts of the attack started when I awoke one night to hear a high pitched sound. I went outside and was shocked to see a large UFO outside the house, seemingly trying to beam a frequency weapon at a person asleep inside. I woke the others in the house and we went into the room where that person was sleeping.

Warren Sunkar

A strange and dark energy pervaded the room and we could feel the presence of something sinister moving in the corner. I have had certain experiences before but this was quite intense, it seemed not to care we were seeing it. Over the years I have worked with various medicines such as ayahuasca and have facilitated various talks and multidimensional experiences, and so know how to basically handle various subtle attacks. However, this being was very persistent and aggressive. We were forced to stay up until late morning keeping the attack at bay until it eventually subsided. However, as we returned exhausted to our bedrooms, in each room was placed some sort of subtle tech device that literally tore up our subtle bodies. We could not enter; they seemed to emit some kind of sick and jarring frequency that wreaked havoc on our internal systems. Over the week we had many visitors who were startled to feel the intensity of these energies.

Over the ensuing days, the attacks persisted with an intensifying ferocity. Those who were with me were shocked at the openness of the attacks. Our country house seemed to become a multidimensional war zone! Portals were opening up, aliens were pouring in from everywhere. After a few nights of not sleeping and being exhausted, I collapsed and a strange event took place…

I was suddenly pulled into a world of beauty and felt free and unencumbered by my dense physical body. This world appealed very much to me, as I stared out to a beautiful horizon of scenic wonders. Yet my deeper being sensed something was very wrong. Despite the landscape of wonder that had opened before me, I centred myself. Everything then became pixelated as if looking at a TV screen. I was in a digitised reality and I looked down at my subtle bodies to see them covered in some kind of subtle tech that had reconfigured my meridians and chakras. I had been implanted with various sophisticated devices within my etheric body when I had passed out. I strained and exerted myself to pull inwardly free, breaking the connection. My consciousness now liberated I opened my eyes to find myself back in the room where I had passed out.

I was quite shaken and discovered that another person in the room had just gone through the same experience. Entering a created virtual reality world has given me the experience and understanding as to how we as a race will possibly be persuaded or forced into one.

Most of the population do not question the reality that surrounds them. We have been subject to fluoridation, vaccines, chemtrails, poisonous food additives. Though most of the Truther Community have been made aware of this, most of the human race is still quite disconnected from nature and their subtle realities. Many are unable to energetically discern the governing and manipulative realities that lie behind civilization's facade. Also, over generations, many people have been encoded with a religious expectation or possibility (this includes a New Age program) of the time we are now facing. In such confusion we will find that we have been primed for a fake saviour, second coming and an Armageddon-like scenario.

The words of writer and transhumanist lecturer Sadiki Bakari stand out in my mind as he points out 'is it going to be a holographic messiah'?

The nature of subtle reality is higher frequencies and energies, mostly unregistered by a material- bound humanity. We as a race have neglected our true psychic heritage through reliance on technocracy. While people jeer at others attempting to share such valuable insight (and despite much New Age glamour) one can only sound a sincere warning here.

While most people look out only to three-dimensional experience, very few would understand that alien technologies, as well as the aliens themselves, can exert influence through fourth-dimensional reality. My various experiences over those ten days made me understand that the subtle technology the Greys have include cloaking devices for themselves and their spacecraft and frequency beams that attack one's DNA. They were able to project a frequency through my body that felt almost beautiful and rapturous, they could use their technology to alter dream states, moods and simulate a seemingly omniscient mental voice, almost like a false Messiah.

I have thought deeply since these experiences. It

would not take much in the coming years to trick a wayward humanity using fear, confusion and war (perhaps a fake alien invasion) to accept a created digital, holographic reality, which to those who are spiritually blind, would seem like a new Heaven. One can see where this writer is going.

We as a race must become aware that interfacing with digital AI is a wormhole to inorganic reality. They have provided us with their own miscreant and subversive technologies. These Greys are capturing and loading our personality consciousness into their created virtual world, while manipulating the human mind into destroying and geo-engineering the Earth. While the world is seemingly getting sicker, the Greys are manipulating us into a controlled digital prison.

I would point out that at the moment most of conditioned humanity would be quite willing to enter.

One of the more worrying trends of the Truther Community is the misunderstanding of what is going on with the planet at present. Their idealism and glamour of divinity have left them extremely vulnerable to false representation. Without true gnosis even the more adept researchers could possibly lead an awakening humanity through a false vortex. True divine experience is rare in this world, despite the glamour of the New Age community. Even those more adept, will find the coming period very difficult because it seems the Greys can even hijack, piggyback and interfere with divine frequencies.

The more powerful attacks eventually subsided; we were aided by divine cosmic intelligence. However, more subtle attacks have continued. Since writing my first two pieces for these essays, I would let you know of another happening just a few weeks ago...

Upon waking, it was still very early in the morning, I went outside to roll some tobacco when I felt an alien presence. However, its approach was now very different to the previous attacks that I had experienced only weeks before. It seemed to project a lighter frequency which felt quite favourable to the personality and which would seem quite beautiful to those inexperienced in such things. But I knew its deception. A Grey semi-materialised before me and spoke to me psychically. It offered me a 'world of my own' where I would not suffer with the rest of humanity if I chose to acquiesce to their plans. I told it to get lost.

Their attacks revealed their true intentions and have left me with some insight into their schemes. However, it made me think how many others may have been offered and given deals. How many in government, the film industry and financial places of power have turned compliant with their wishes out of fear, confusion and even misplaced intentions?

With the ongoing and current awakening of the human race we will find that we might possibly have to navigate through a hostile multidimensional experience. However, there is much hope here because we as divine representatives have the definite capacity to deal with such situations. We never need to acquiesce to alien intelligence. Our own divine heritage and alignment is sound and if we invoke through our lives true divinity, our capability exceeds that of these lost and wayward beings.

Living in true alignment we never need be afraid when we encounter such things, and I'm sure in the not too distant future…we might be forced to!

Pokemon No!
It's All Going a Bit Grey – Part 4

Not long ago, humanity thought it strange or simply did not know that micro-organisms were part of our reality until the invention of the microscope. Now accepted as fact, it is worth pondering how much we miss in terms of intelligent life outside of our visible spectrum of reality. With the planetary shift under way, many people are experiencing multidimensional awakening and cosmic realignment, opening them up to various subtle realities and experiences.

What has been hidden is now being revealed.

My experiences over the past few months have highlighted planetary manipulation from entities of alien origin, known by some people today as the Greys. Having recently experienced and seen their various subtle technologies – such as bio-etheric implants, frequency jamming devices, manipulative frequency technologies that influence the subconscious mind, cloaking devices for themselves and their vehicles, subtle architecture placed in certain locations around the planet and a complete augmented reality – it seems high government officials and elites are either knowingly or unknowingly compliant with their schemes. Also, people such as scientists, doctors and politicians who are predominantly left-brained can be easily corrupted and infiltrated through their minds, becoming unknowing accomplices to their suggestive realities and manipulations.

Today, the reality of psychotronic warfare on individuals and the public is being exposed. Whistle-blowers are coming forward, and corporate patents and documents have been released. This type of technology is itself given or mentally implanted by the Greys who use compatible technology from the more subtle fields of reality they inhabit. Frequency control and manipulation technologies are very real silent weapons of war being used against humanity and are affecting the collective in many adverse ways.

There is also a heavy assault on human biology as well as much engineered social confusion. Despite the dangers of EMF exposure, weather modification, bio-engineering and GM food, today's transhumanist agenda is being pushed ahead by certain authorities in spite of any objections. The public in their ignorance are often used to further the agenda, and 'modern life' is being deviously crafted in such a way so as to make existence without phones, computers, tablets etc. impossible!

While many people are seeking to inform the public about the growing dangers of our technocratic reality, Hollywood propaganda films, such as *Transcedence,* often highlight a programing of hostility and exaggeration towards those people who are telling others to unplug, making them out as terrorists, unintelligent, or backwards.

Those of us who live in genuine empathic connection to our Mother Earth and our cosmic realities can plainly see the great harm that all of this is doing from our more subtle perspectives and insight. Our cities and people have mostly lost sympathetic resonance with their natural and spiritual environments. Too few people understand that Mother Earth has her own consciousness and life processes, and that we through our biology and energetic composition share the current cosmic alignment and ascension process with her.

There is a great obscuration of understanding as to what we as a race view as technology. We have come into a great neglect of our true psychic and spiritual realities. Instead of working with our natural and cosmic realities we seek to oppose them. This is a sickness of spirit exemplified in rampant materialism, selfishness and domination of lower patriarchal impulses. This is the great curse of the domineering collective Western mindset.

As we delve deeper into misaligned and augmented reality, we are opening ourselves to greater possession and parasitic infection from rogue elements in the cosmos. The Greys are using subtle implant devices and controlled frequency fields to eventually take over and possess an unsuspecting society. Those in high-tech EMF environments, such as the military and police, are much more susceptible to possession or influence due to their conditioning, as well as drug users and gamers who have weak resistance. I would point out that some of these random killings and shootings we are seeing today are in fact AI possession, orchestrated from the subtle realms to keep the public in fear and low vibratory frequency.

While writing these pieces we have seen the advent of a new gaming in the guise of Pokémon Go. This enables people using GPS and Wi-Fi to travel to various locations around the planet to participate in capturing virtual animals. While the argument is that it is getting people outdoors, it is the inverse nature of interacting with our natural environment that needs to be highlighted. I watched hundreds of people at a well-known park in my city trample the earth and vegetation in an effort to retrieve Pokémon, each with their 'smart' phone on, with little respect for the grounds they trudged through (this park is considered sacred by our indigenous brothers and sisters). The wildlife and flowers were neglected and trashed for virtual ones.

The energetic nature of our being shares reciprocal energetic interfacing and connection with our spiritual and biological environments. How we live and what we live for is what we invoke as our experience in our given reality. Energy can be siphoned off-planet by reverse energy grid networks to off-planetary recipients. These grids have been constructed and engineered at fourth and fifth- dimensional levels by various alien entities. I would point out that while many Truthers focus on the social implications and subversive intelligence tactics of the technology behind such games as Pokémon Go, perhaps it is pertinent to present the possibility of energetic harvesting and complete consciousness bilocation.

Unaware of subtle realities, people do not understand that there are various technologies placed around the planet in different frequencies of reality. These create inverse fields that are being used by the Greys to open certain portals that subdue the population's consciousness into their virtual reality framework. Many people are today literally walking through this portal and are being assimilated by alien artificial intelligence.

On a deeper level, many servers are today experiencing the deep levels of planetary manipulation and trauma that have existed in more unconscious levels of planetary experience. This is a transmutational process to heal and rectify those unseen and unknown elements that have affected the human race for millennia. Some of us may encounter hostile alien realities through this period of planetary transformation. Many of these hostile alien realities are losing ground and becoming desperate as the deeper cleansing of the planet proceeds. Like myself, you might encounter attacks, infiltrations and implanting through this period.

While the world is seemingly collapsing into madness as dualities within the collective human psyche are being exacerbated and brought to the surface, we are called to hold our alignment in faith through these planetary processes. We have much divine assistance and this is an important period to resolve certain elements of the planetary fracturing. It is also a parting of ways.

As new cosmic energies sweep into this sphere, humanity will possibly encounter those deeper layers of collective psyche which will expunge fractured realities and heal our inherent individual cleavages to reveal how, as a race, we are subject to archonic infiltration. This is part of the planetary purgation process and will allow those of the race who are walking the path to clear various internal and external obstructions and implants, helping us to understand how AI infiltration is taking place. For people who are unable to integrate with the new frequencies this could be akin to a planetary dark night.

The true seed is today being removed from the husk. I can say with experience and certainty that these miscreant alien intelligences are failing in their schemes despite the seeming chaos on a planetary level.

Our planetary Mother has been under great pressure. I cannot stress the importance for people to go deeper in their search for truth. With our cosmic realignment taking place today only those who truly seek spiritual integration will know what is taking place behind the veil of confusion that is confronting us on every level of our earthly experience. Despite the madness, the attacks, the hostility of a wayward world, one can only smile at what is revealing itself on deeper levels of being.

To the Great Universal Mother I give reverence and thanks!

THIS TIME OF CHANGE

If we viewed ancient cultures with more respect for their inherent mental integrity, we might discover the logic behind some of their spiritual beliefs and practices and realize that such practices might have advanced scientific validity at their core. If we begin to validate the contours of the ancient psyche we would begin to comprehend more about the workings of the contemporary mind and would perhaps not jump to the conclusion that people are mentally disturbed simply because they have extraordinary experiences. We might discover that extraordinary experiences are the result of perceptional evolution. Once we collectively advance to a more evolved state of consciousness, extra-ordinary experiences, such as contact with inhabitants of Otherworlds, might become quite ordinary.
   Voyagers- A. Deane.

In alignment with current planetary shifts, humanity is quickly assimilating new energies and encodings that are changing how they presently perceive their reality.

Warren Sunkar

We live in a period of acceleration in regards to planetary ascension processes and the expansion of global consciousness. With the emergence of multi-dimensional awareness in portions of humanity comes the unfolding recognition that what we have perceived as 'reality' is but a very limited spectrum of consciousness and that the physical material realm is the small visible arena of a much bigger multidimensional landscape that most of humanity is unaware of.

But this is nothing new.

Over the age certain ancient cultures and mystics also pointed out that we as humans are capable of embodying experiences that surpass our mundane realities. They gave knowledge of other worlds and teachings of divine initiation. They also pointed to the cosmological events that were leading us to this time of great change.

Now with the more recent advancements of quantum physics and space travel, we have initiated the exploration into interdimensional physics and in conjunction with the contemporary new age movement we have just started to validate the greater application of scientific laws as to how they correlate and apply to human spirituality. With these emergent understandings new possibilities are opening up for us as a race that are also having us re-discover hidden secrets about our ancient past by which our current belief systems will be progressively overturned. What we are presently experiencing is just the beginning and with this rapid evolution of consciousness these refreshed perspectives are leading us to a synthesis of historical and modern belief systems, of science and spirituality which is coalescing into an expanding new model of consciousness that is inviting us into a new paradigm.

For quite a long time it seems, general human awareness has been mostly chained to the physical/material realm and our consciousness has been mostly earthbound. This fixation of perception has greatly clouded our assessments and has had us miss and confuse many things about the true nature of the universe. It is just over recent decades that we have begun to comprehend the holographic nature of reality and now that humanity is venturing deeper out into space we have only just started to leave our gross relativities to explore concepts and theories beyond the limitations of our mundane tellurian perspectives. We are today acknowledging that life is not bound to our own limited spectrums and dimensions of reality.

In these times of rapid awakening we will need to have the courage, wisdom and resilience to witness the new as it emerges. As we all journey together beyond the boundaries of our material rationalisations we also start to become more receptive to influences from other dimensional realities that are unknown and untouched by present sciences. As these new vistas of experience open, we will open the door to the meta-physical and discover our greater potentialities as a race. As more people turn on their inherent multidimensional capacities in line with ascending planetary processes they will increasingly witness and experience contact with other dimensional realties and beings by which the very foundations of contempory scientific, religious, historical and cultural beliefs will be shaken. These experiences will have us needfully re-evaluate everything.

Throughout human history there have been legends and myths about visitors from ancient worlds. They were often called angels, demons and 'Gods from the sky,' – today we hear of growing sightings of UFO's and contact with extra-terrestrial beings. With our current shifts of consciousness, contemporary humanity is only beginning to comprehend that there are many other realities present all around us but we have been incapable of observing them. We are awakening to the fact that we share our world with many unseen beings and that our universe is filled with many diverse life forms, intelligences and realities that inhabit planes and dimensions beyond the physical. That just because a planet looks uninhabited from our gross perspectives does not mean it does not have life on other dimensional levels of its reality. We are also realising that some of these extra-terrestrial beings have been visiting Earth over untold millennia and today quietly walk amongst us. In this time of planetary ascension things are fast changing and we as a race are being forced to confront this new multi-dimensional terrain.

However, when we hear the words 'extra-terrestrial' or 'angel' they are just common words and generalised identifications that usually have very little scientific merit and have not been publicly subject to any deeper analysis. As growing awareness of extra-terrestrial intelligence becomes increasingly acknowledged by the general population, people will find that these words do not suitably identify or explain the differences of classes that make up the great host of divergent intelligences and beings that many people from around the world have been observing. They do not clarify the differences in matter density, biological make up and consciousness levels these beings exhibit nor do they help us to understand the historic relationships we may share with them. To better comprehend all of this, we will have to expand our minds enough to fathom the greater multidimensional framework that we all share beyond our currently limited and linear time/space educational models.

With ET disclosure our belief systems will be radically modified and we will progressively start to observe reconciliation between both ancient esoteric and modern scientific perspectives. Eventually this will have us understand that science and spirituality were never opposing realities but two sides of the one coin. That in our true evolution into interdimensional sciences and theory we must incorporate both universal physics and spiritual insight because only working together will these disciplines emerge as the sacred sciences that are needed to safely open the hidden door to our multi-dimensional cosmic reality. Our new perceptions will increasingly reveal the fallacies, distortions and hidden truths of both creationism and evolutionary Darwinism to ultimately bring us into a new era of higher understanding.

At present, there is a real need for this.

As we observe the increasing chaos and troubles that are engulfing the world today, more people will progressively comprehend that most of the causes of human suffering and confusion are coming from levels of reality that they do not know about or yet understand. Much has been hidden from humanity and with rising awareness of secretive government collaboration with off-world intelligence, more people than ever will begin to question the narratives that have shaped our worldly belief systems. We might just discover that many of the global problems that we face have an alien causation!

This comprehension will lead us into new and unexpected spheres of reasoning and inquiry that will prove valuable in coming years but it will take much courage to unlock these doors of perception and wisdom to navigate these new domains.

As the world responds to the new frequencies of energy that are becoming available to the planet we will unearth many things. We will realise that our true earth history is very different to what we have been led to believe. In our expanding vision of reality we will need to incorporate many new and otherworldly perspectives to understand who and what we are in the greater scheme of cosmic life. These revelations may be startling and confusing but we also need to comprehend that we have the ability to overcome whatever may be put in front of us

These realisations also have the potential to help us to reinvent a much better relationship with each other and the Earth because over the age we have forgotten so much. As we re-discover the truths of our forgotten cosmic ancestry we might just find out that we may share certain genetic relationships with some of the extra-terrestrial beings. This knowledge will change our fundamental assumptions of reality to eventually reveal that our true divine heritage is more beautiful and magnificent than what we have ever thought possible.

Welcome to the future…

Open The Window of Grace

In this global society of technocratic convenience, entertainment and selfish distraction, how few people take time to still and truly gain the needed moments and space to open, bringing about the deeper inner clarity and transcendental awareness to assist a world that is seemingly spinning out of control? How few people even care or see the necessity of doing so?

Within today's great collective confusion and troubles, there is so much needed to be said about sacredness!

Sacredness reveals itself in the purity of relationships that are formed with God, ourselves and the planet. When we know true sacredness, we open our hearts and minds to the guidance and subtle caress of divine Life and we are drawn into Love's presence. Sacredness is the vehicle through which we come to understand our true nature and we come to realise that we are constantly showered with God's unspeakable blessings. Here, in awe of Life, we are constantly falling to our knees and can behold 'Truth Unmanifest' through our open window of reverence and love. Here, within the sacredness of a moment, Love manifests to touch our hearts as do the kisses of the morning sun's rays for those who awaken early to receive them.

It is through the portal of sacredness that we experience a constant renewal in Life...

If you would but take that little time you have to contemplate this, you would understand that this is what lies in sacredness!

Sacredness is not an ideal or a concept. It is the inspired reverence you bring to the moment you are living. People should understand that true divine blessing can be experienced everywhere and in any situation but that we must offer ourselves up in sincerity and love. Sacredness is lived in the true recognition of divinity that pervades all form, through whatever place, being or moment we are interacting with. When Life is revered and we as a people come to honour each other in respect to our divine nature then this creates the opportunity for Spirit to teach and bless us. We then come to know Life consciously and know the purpose of our being!

Our modern culture for the most part has lost its sense of sacredness and does not recognise its importance. Without it, we lose our fundamental connection to essential reality and sensitiveness to those sublime understandings and elements that are given to us by Life to truly guide and nourish us. Without sacredness and respect for the divine Life we lose our spiritual guidance and begin to venerate matter and form. We become lost in dualistic reality and fall deeper into the illusions of self.

Today, this world has plunged deep into a material abyss of self-gratification, and we are seeing the direct results. In the degradation of true culture and our relationships to each other and the Earth, sciences and the arts, potential tools used to elevate and enliven the race have become so polluted and degenerate their effect on society only weakens and defiles it. Driven by the chaos of their personality, people seal themselves from the true understanding of Life. This is true blindness!

When we lose sacredness we lose our divine compass and in our confusion we fall deeper from what sustains us. Our inspired recognition of the sacredness of Life opens the portal to higher dimensional reality. The opposite is also very true; in denial and negligence of Spirit we find ourselves lost in psychosis, trapped in misery and fear. As our society falls deeper into materialism and thus into madness we see the fires of hell arise around us in confusion, depression, vampirism and war.

We see this sickness arising in today's incessant push of those technocratic and inorganic pathways towards spiritless realities and worlds. Today our culture, has become a celebration of debasement and much of today's society is resembling the demonic stories of old!

Most people interact with each other and the planet

in a semiconscious daze, seeking only the attainment of their own desires and needs. Humanity is today cloaked with heavy insatiable elementals of their personality and it is here that they open themselves to be controlled by darker entities and beings. Collectively they are being driven off a metaphysical cliff to plunge into an even deeper abyss of hatred, conflict, and brutality...

Yet if we could only just open and trust our sense of sacredness it could elevate us far beyond the dangers and miseries of our prevailing conditions.

Let one here ask:

How few people today consciously engage in life with the love and clarity that is aroused by Spirit?

How few people are even able to recognise the importance and necessity to see the sacredness in Life?

When you walk in nature do you take time to be still and feel her presence?

When you look into the eyes of the opposite sex do you honour their soul with your integrity and truth?

Is your walk through life attempting to live the deepest truths that reveal themselves to your heart, and how do you live behind closed doors?

When you know the sacredness in all things your answer will be without fear, confusion or hesitation.

Today as we watch in awe at that which is rising before us, let us see clearly the tragedy of our modern culture and look deeply inside ourselves. Then we ourselves have the opportunity to see the sacredness of this moment in our planetary collective history. To turn this moment into the greatest of blessings and meet divine Truth face to face. Then we can honour God, ourselves and our brothers and sisters by holding our alignment, integrity and truth before them. This is true divine work.

We must not only remember but live in sacredness... this moment is sacred, the Earth is sacred, humanity is sacred. When you know such a Reality and Love then your very lives become a divine blessing upon the world.

Verily, the whole cosmos will sing with you!

The Changing of Days, The Parting of Ways

Many today are experiencing and benefitting from the new living energies that are presently entering our planet. The great change is here and humanity is expanding into a multidimensional consciousness and reality that now awakens us to our true cosmic origins and shifts us into an energetically regenerative ascending cycle of divine possibility.

At this time we are also witnessing the birth of the *new race*.

These emerging children of Life have the inherent capacities to adapt to our fast changing energetic environment and bring with them the ability to greatly assist humanity in this time of radical transformation and change.

Those more astute understand these incoming energies offer a profound opportunity for healing the deep fractures within our personal and collective being.

How people experience the current waves of grace depends on their own choices.

These subtle living energies are able to be received by those who are truly seeking alignment and living by their purist and truest standards of being.

People are now coming to the realisation that the emergent new reality is in fact already here but it is still unnoticed by the majority.

The conditioned impetus of modern life is still dominating upon a self-centred collective.

While many people are sensing that things are changing, few are able to comprehend the true nature of these changes. We are being called to let go of a paradigm that no longer serves our inherent life purpose, and those who remain clinging to a degenerating and self-centred social template will find themselves unprepared as these energies intensify.

And they will now continue to dramatically intensify!

These living energies require the participation of our entire being. It is possible that the recognition of the emergent new life will be neglected and even repudiated for a short while but this will not go on indefinitely. Everyone will soon be unable to deny the energies and changes the new life is generating.

Contextual parameters are being adjusted and conceptual realities dissolved in the light of the new day. People need to let go of those belief structures and programed expectations of what the new cycle is to bring.

Nothing of the old can enter the new!

As the Earth reconfigures, we will experience open communication with the living cosmos and the multitude of life expressions therein. Our new multidimensional configurations with our mutating DNA are receiving new light encodings that are now ultimately leading us to a complete review of our current planetary status.

Humanity is now discovering that it is certainly not alone in this universe!

This is leading to a new assessment of earth's history as we come to understand the true nature of our terrestrial environment as well as our cosmic lineages.

Today we are witnessing a clearing of artificial timelines and patterns, the removal of parasitical realities and we are being provided with a more accessible means to awaken our true divine potentiality.

The earth alignment and healing is an ongoing process that will give an awakening humanity a greater inherent connectivity and a more expansive frequency range of experience to ultimately connect it with its true divine source.

Today a bifurcation of realities is occurring between those who are choosing to integrate and align with the new divine energies that are entering the planet and those who refuse to change their selfish ways.

Those who continue to hold on to the diminishing and fading paradigm will find their lives will continue to become much harder until they mend their errant ways or face possible assimilation by artificial intelligence and leave the planet altogether.

This world cannot continue in its current misalignments.

Humanity, it is overtime to turn off your computers and throw out your televisions.

Allow the living intelligence of Life to guide you through the great changes of the day.

The time is Now!

www.ingramcontent.com/pod-product-compliance
Lightning Source LLC
Chambersburg PA
CBHW070631300426
44113CB00010B/1738